W9-ASR-885

EXPLORING WORLD CULTURES

Turkey

Joanne Mattern

Cavendish
Square

New York

Published in 2019 by Cavendish Square Publishing, LLC
243 5th Avenue, Suite 136, New York, NY 10016

Copyright © 2019 by Cavendish Square Publishing, LLC

First Edition

No part of this publication may be reproduced, stored in a retrieval system, or transmitted in any form or by any means—electronic, mechanical, photocopying, recording, or otherwise—without the prior permission of the copyright owner. Request for permission should be addressed to Permissions, Cavendish Square Publishing, 243 5th Avenue, Suite 136, New York, NY 10016. Tel (877) 980-4450; fax (877) 980-4454.

Website: cavendishsq.com

This publication represents the opinions and views of the author based on his or her personal experience, knowledge, and research. The information in this book serves as a general guide only. The author and publisher have used their best efforts in preparing this book and disclaim liability rising directly or indirectly from the use and application of this book.

All websites were available and accurate when this book was sent to press.

Library of Congress Cataloging-in-Publication Data

Names: Mattern, Joanne, 1963- author.
Title: Turkey / Joanne Mattern.
Description: First edition. | New York, NY : Cavendish Square Publishing, LLC, 2018. | Series: Exploring world cultures | Includes bibliographical references and index.
Identifiers: LCCN 2017048058 (print) | LCCN 2017052775 (ebook) | ISBN 9781502638212 (ebook) | ISBN 9781502638182 (library bound) | ISBN 9781502638199 (pbk.) | ISBN 9781502638205 (6 pack)
Subjects: LCSH: Turkey--Juvenile literature.
Classification: LCC DR417.4 (ebook) | LCC DR417.4 .M37 2018 (print) | DDC 956.1--dc23
LC record available at https://lccn.loc.gov/2017048058

Editorial Director: David McNamara
Editor: Jodyanne Benson
Copy Editor: Rebecca Rohan
Associate Art Director: Amy Greenan
Designer: Christina Shults
Production Coordinator: Karol Szymczuk
Photo Research: J8 Media

The photographs in this book are used by permission and through the courtesy of: Cover Cindy Hopkin/Alamy Stock Photo; p. 5 Byelikova Oksana/Shutterstock.com; p. 6 Dikobraziy/Shutterstock.com; p. 7 Malcolm P Chapman/Moment/Getty Images; p. 8 Keystone/Hulton Archive/Getty Images; p. 9 Ilyas Akengin/AFP/Getty Images; p. 10 Adem Altan/AFP/Getty Images; p. 11 Orhan Cam/Shutterstock.com; p. 12 Andrew Rowat/Corbis/Getty Images; p. 13 Yulia Grigoryeva/Shutterstock.com; p. 14 Murat Oner Tas/Anadolu Agency/Getty Images; p. 15 Ondrej Prosicky/Shutterstock.com; p. 16 Janine Wiedel Photolibrary/Alamy Stock Photo; p. 18 Terrance Klassen/Age Fotostock/Getty Images; p. 19/Corbis/Getty Images; p 20 deepspace/Shutterstock.com; p. 21 Khaled ElAdawy/Shutterstock.com; p. 22 Michele Burgess/Alamy Stock Photo; 24 Florin1961/iStockphoto.com; p. 26 Izzet Keribar/Lonely Planet Images/Getty Images; p. 27 Tahsinaydogmus/iStock/Thinkstock; p. 28 Tahsinaydogmus/Shutterstock.com; p. 29 Africa Studio/Shutterstock.com.

Printed in the United States of America

Contents

Turkey is one country on two continents. Most of Turkey is in Asia. A small part of Turkey is in Europe. Most of Turkey is surrounded by water. The eastern and western parts of the country are bordered by land.

Turkey has many different landscapes. The country has high mountains. It also has **plateaus**. There are beautiful beaches along the coast. Turkey is home to many busy cities. Istanbul is one of the most beautiful and busiest cities in the world.

More than eighty million people live in Turkey. Most Turks are Muslims. Members of other faiths also live in Turkey.

Turkey has a long history. Like people everywhere, Turks enjoy good times with family and friends. They enjoy sports and games. They work and go to school. Turkey is a beautiful nation that is home to many interesting stories.

Crowds pack a street in Istanbul, one of the busiest cities in the world.

Geography

Turkey covers 302,535 square miles (783,562 square kilometers). The Black Sea borders Turkey's northern coast. The Mediterranean Sea borders the country to the south. The Aegean Sea borders

This map shows Turkey and the countries and bodies of water around it.

the western part of Turkey. Part of western Turkey borders Bulgaria and Greece. In the east, Turkey borders Georgia, Armenia, Azerbaijan, and Iran. Part of southern Turkey borders Iraq and Syria.

Mount Ararat is the tallest mountain in Turkey. It is actually a **dormant** volcano.

White Stone

Pamukkale is an area of high cliffs in western Turkey. The cliffs are covered with a white mineral called calcite.

Most of Turkey is in Asia. This part of the nation is called Anatolia. Anatolia has mountains and plateaus. Two important rivers are the Tigris

Pamukkale means "cotton castle."

and the Euphrates. They flow through eastern and southern Turkey.

A narrow strip of water separates Asian Turkey from European Turkey. This water is called the Turkish Straits. Because Turkey is a **peninsula**, it has many beautiful beaches. Turkey also has **fertile** land and thick forests.

7

History

The earliest people who lived in Anatolia were the Hittites. They lived there as far back as the seventeenth century BCE. Later, Persians ruled Anatolia. Then, in 334 BCE, Alexander the Great came from Greece and conquered Anatolia.

Atatürk was the first leader of modern Turkey.

After Alexander the Great died, the Romans controlled Anatolia. Much later, the Seljuq Turks arrived from central Asia. They gained control of the nation. In the 1200s, the Mongols invaded Anatolia. They created the mighty Ottoman Empire.

FACT!

St. Nicholas was a Christian bishop who lived in Turkey. He cared for the poor and sick.

The Ottoman Empire lasted until the end of World War I. After the war, the area became Turkey. Turkey's new leader and first president, Mustafa Kemal Atatürk, introduced modern customs. He made a nonreligious government.

Over the years, Turkey has seen weak governments. There have been fights between the Turks and the government, too. Today, Turkey still struggles with government and religious issues.

Children wave the Turkish flag to support the army.

The Young Turks

In 1908, a group of students and military leaders forced the **sultan** out of power. This group was called the Young Turks.

VOTE ✓

Turkey's government has three branches. The president and the prime minister make up the executive branch. The prime minister leads a council of ministers. Ministers head departments for foreign affairs, finance, tourism, and more.

The Grand National Assembly meets to vote on an issue.

The Grand National Assembly makes up the legislative branch. The assembly has 550 members. Members are elected to four-year terms.

Turkey's president is elected by the people. He or she serves a five-year term.

Their main job is to make laws. The Assembly can also declare war.

The judicial branch enforces the law. The Constitutional Court decides whether laws are correct. The Court of Cassation reviews criminal cases from lower courts.

Turkey is divided into eighty-one provinces. Each province is ruled by a governor. Provinces are divided into smaller counties, districts, and villages.

Turkish flags fly in front of the Foreign Affairs Building in Ankara.

Turkey's Capital

Ankara is the capital of Turkey. About 3.5 million people live there.

The Economy

At one time, most of the people in Turkey were farmers. Today, only about 25 percent of Turks work in agriculture. Turkey produces many crops. The nation's top crops include

A waiter prepares for tourists at a fancy restaurant on the water in Istanbul.

cherries, figs, apricots, hazelnuts, and tomatoes. Vegetables such as cucumbers, eggplants, and peppers are also popular.

Many beautiful flowers grow in Turkey. About one-quarter of the roses in the world come from Turkey.

FACT!

Turkish farmers also raise cattle, sheep, goats, and water buffalo.

The Land of Lira

Turkish money is called lira. In 2017, one Turkish lira equaled about thirty American cents.

Turkish lira features pictures of important Turkish leaders.

About 45 percent of Turks work in the service industry. They work in transportation, stores, hotels, and banks. Tourists come from all over the world to visit Turkey. So, tourism is an important part of the economy.

About 25 percent of Turkey's economy is manufacturing. Turkey's factories produce cars and heavy machinery. They also produce clothing, chemicals, and electronics.

The Environment

About 15 percent of Turkey is covered with forests. Chestnut, pine, and sycamore trees grow in the northwest. Oaks and maples grow in the mountains near the Black Sea. Olive and licorice trees grow in the southeast.

Tulips were first grown in Turkey many years ago.

Many beautiful flowers grow in Turkey. The national flower is the tulip. Turkey also has many lilies, roses, and poppies.

In 2010, Turkey created the first wildlife **corridor** to protect animals.

A Paradise for Animals

Hundreds of birds live in Turkey. The number grows even more in the spring. That's when birds **migrate** from Africa to Asia and Europe.

Turkey is home to many different animals. Large mammals include bears, wolves, and lynx. Gazelles and mountain goats live in the mountains. More than 120 different kinds of snakes, lizards, and tortoises also live there.

You can find beautiful flamingos standing tall in Turkish lakes.

The seas around Turkey are full of fish. Loggerhead turtles, monk seals, and squid also swim in Turkey's seas.

The People Today

Turkey's population is about eighty million. There are many different **ethnic** groups in Turkey. Many people have come from other countries to live in Turkey. About three-quarters of Turkey's population are ethnic Turks. They have lived in the area for a thousand years.

A family enjoys a Mother's Day picnic at a park in Turkey.

FACT!

Beginning in 2015, many people from Syria came to Turkey to escape war.

Fighting for Rights

For many years, Kurds have been treated badly in Turkey. Many Kurds would like to form their own separate nation.

The second largest population in Turkey are Kurds. They make up about 20 percent of the nation. Kurds live in eastern Turkey. At one time, many Kurds were **nomads** who herded sheep and goats.

Other ethnic groups in Turkey include Arabs, Greeks, and Armenians.

Today, more people from other countries move to the big cities in Turkey. This means that it is more common for people of different ethnicities to get married.

Lifestyle

Most Turks live in cities. Istanbul is the largest city in Turkey. More than eleven million people live there. The city is very crowded and noisy. Most people live in apartments. Many stores line the crowded streets.

Apartments crowd the streets of Istanbul.

Some people live in villages or on farms. These areas have stone or brick houses.

Turkish children go to school when they are six years old. They go to school for twelve years.

FACT!

Istanbul's Grand Bazaar is one of the largest covered markets in the world.

Going to College

There are 174 universities and colleges in Turkey. Istanbul University was founded in 1453. It has more than eighty thousand students.

Students study many different subjects. There are two kinds of high schools. One kind prepares students for college. The other prepares students for a trade, such as building or repairing cars.

Students are working together in a class at Istanbul Bilgi University.

Women have not always had the same opportunities as men in Turkey. Today, Turkish women have more rights. They are even becoming more involved in government.

Religion

Religion is very important in Turkey. Most Turks are Muslims. They follow a religion called Islam. Muslims pray in buildings called mosques. There are thousands of mosques in Turkey. Most Muslims in Turkey

Men gather to pray at Turkey's Blue Mosque during Ramadan.

are Sunni Muslims. There is also a different group called Shia Muslims. Another group of Muslims is called Sufi. Sufism focuses on inner peace.

There are also many Christians in Turkey. Christianity began thousands of years ago.

Muslims have to pray five times a day.

Separating Church and State

At one time, Turkish laws followed religious teaching. Atatürk changed that. Today, the church and the state are separate.

There are many historical Christian cities in Turkey, including Antioch. Many missions in the Bible took place in these Turkish cities. Today, about 45,000 Turks belong to the Armenian Apostolic Church. Other Christian churches include the Eastern Orthodox Church and the Syriac Orthodox Church. There are also Catholics and Protestants.

St. Anthony of Padua is a Roman Catholic Church in Istanbul.

Language

Most people in Turkey speak Turkish. Turkish is a lot like Arabic and Persian languages. In the past, Turkish was written in the Arabic alphabet. When Atatürk came to power, he wanted to make Turkey more modern. In 1928, he

BİLET GİŞESİ
(Ticket Office)
DEYRULZAFARAN MANASTIRI
(Deyrulzafaran Monastery)
GİRİŞ ÜCRETİ (Admission Fee)

TAM BİLET (Full Ticket) : 5 TL
ÖĞRENCİ BİLETİ (Student Ticket) : 3 TL

This entrance sign features directions in both English and Turkish.

changed the official alphabet to Latin. The new Turkish alphabet had twenty-nine letters. It is a lot like the English alphabet.

The Kurds have their own language. It is called Kurmānjī. Kurmānjī is also spoken by Kurds who live in Iran, Iraq, and Syria.

FACT!

The Turkish alphabet does not have the letters q, w, or x.

Because it is close to the Arab countries, some people in southeastern Turkey speak Arabic. However, Turkish is taught in schools. People who speak other languages can usually speak Turkish as well.

A Quick Change

Atatürk only gave people six months to change from the Arabic alphabet to the Latin alphabet.

23

Music and dancing are very popular in Turkey. There are many music festivals in the summer. Turks like all kinds of music. They listen to everything from classical to pop music. Traditional folk music and dancing are often enjoyed at weddings and festivals.

Turkish dancers wear traditional costumes at an international folk festival.

Turks have created beautiful works of art. Palaces and mosques are usually decorated with brightly colored tiles. Turks also weave rugs and **tapestries**. Other artists create paintings, pottery, and sculptures.

Most people in Turkey celebrate Ramadan and other Muslim holidays. During the month of Ramadan, people do not eat between sunrise and sunset.

Turks celebrate many different holidays. National Sovereignty Day and Republic Day honor Atatürk. So does Atatürk Day. Turks also celebrate Children's Day and Youth and Sports Day.

Wonderful Stories

Turkey has a long history of great literature. Ancient writers created poems and fables. Modern writers create popular novels and plays.

Fun and Play

There are a lot of ways to have fun in Turkey. People in Turkey enjoy many different sports. Soccer is the most popular sport. Turks also enjoy basketball and wrestling. In the winter, many people enjoy skiing in the snowy mountains.

Backgammon is a favorite way to pass the time in Turkey.

Water sports are also very popular. People enjoy swimming, scuba diving,

FACT!

Naim Süleymanoğlu is a weightlifter who has won three Olympic gold medals. He is called Pocket Hercules because he is less than five feet tall!

An Unusual Sport

The Camel Wrestling Championship is held in Selçuk, Turkey, every year. The camels push and lean against each other until one falls or just walks away.

Camels face off during a wrestling match.

and canoeing. There are activities for any time of the year.

Turks enjoy getting together for games. Backgammon is a very popular board game. Players often gather in teahouses to play games and drink hot tea. Turks also enjoy going to concerts, movies, and plays.

Food

People in Turkey love food! Cheese and olives are often eaten for breakfast. Lunch might include soup, pasta, or rice. Dinner is the biggest meal of the day. Dinner can start with soups and salads. These are followed by lamb, chicken, or beef served with rice. A wheat grain called bulgar is also popular.

A kebab chef prepares a traditional Turkish street food.

Seafood is a popular dish along the coast. People enjoy fish. They also eat octopus, squid, and mussels.

FACT!

The most popular drink in Turkey is tea. People drink it from small glasses with beet sugar.

Sweet Treats

Baklava is a sweet pastry layered with nuts and honey. Another popular dessert is a kind of doughnut called *lokma.*

Shish kebabs are a popular street food. Shish kebabs are meat and vegetables grilled on a long stick. Food vendors also sell fresh almonds or nut breads.

Sweet, flaky baklava is a favorite dessert in Turkey.

Tea is grown in Rize Province on the Black Sea coast. It grows well here because of the mild climate and high precipitation. The soil is also very fertile.

Glossary

corridor   A land path used by migrating animals.

dormant   Not active; sleeping.

ethnic   Related to people who have a common national or cultural tradition.

fertile   Able to produce crops.

migrate   To move from one place to another.

nomads   People who travel from place to place.

peninsula   Land that is surrounded by water on three sides.

plateaus   Areas of flat, raised land.

sultan   A powerful Muslim ruler.

tapestries   Heavy cloths with pictures or patterns woven into them.

Find Out More

Books

Cline, Bev. *Turkey*. New York, NY: AV2 by Weigl, 2015.

Murray, Julie. *Turkey*. Minneapolis, MN: ABDO

    Publishing Company, 2015.

Website

National Geographic Kids: Turkey

http://kids.nationalgeographic.com/explore/

countries/turkey/#turkey-istanbul.jpg

Video

Kids Learning Tube: Country of Turkey

https://www.youtube.com/watch?v=hUweTdyoUss

Index

About the Author

Joanne Mattern is the author of more than 250 books for children. She specializes in writing nonfiction and has explored many different places in her writing. Her favorite topics include history, travel, sports, biography, and animals. Joanne lives in New York State with her husband, four children, and several pets.